Carnivore Air Fryer Cookbook

Crispy, Easy and Healthy Air Fryer Recipes for Meat Lovers

Brence Highter

Table of Contents

Introduction

Do you ever wonder what an all-meat diet is like?

We were told that eating lots of red meat is not good for our body and may even cause life-threatening diseases.

We are encouraged to aim for a balanced diet with an emphasis on lots of fruits and vegetables.

But recent findings suggest that red meat is not as bad as we previously believed. The human body only needs essential vitamins, minerals, fat, and protein. All these are present in animal meat.

If you're a meat-eater or maybe you are planning to take on the carnivore diet, you might want to also consider using an air fryer.

Air fryers have been popular with keto dieters for their ability to cook a wide range of foods for a short amount of time.

Read on for more information about the carnivore diet and the air fryer.

Chapter 1: Overview of the Carnivore Diet

What is the Carnivore Diet?

The carnivore diet is an eating plan that consists exclusively of animal meat and meat products. It excludes all other food items like fruits, vegetables, seeds, legumes, nuts, and others.

List of Carnivore Diet Approved Food

- Red meat, preferably grass-fed and organic (beef, pork, lamb, and game meat)
- Fatty fish (sardines, salmon, mackerel, trout, cod, tilapia, and tuna)
- Seafood (crab, lobster, and shrimp)
- Offal or animal organs (liver, kidneys, tripe, brain, and connective tissues)
- Eggs
- Bone marrow
- Bone soups and broths
- Food seasonings or condiments (salt, pepper, herbs, and spices)
- Fat (lard, butter, and tallow)
- Dairy (milk, cheese, and yogurt)
- Moderate amounts of vegetables

Benefits of the Carnivore Diet

- Weight loss

Our body needs calories to function properly. People on normal non-restrictive diets source calories from a diverse selection of foods and drinks, while people on a carnivore diet get all their caloric needs from the fat and protein in the animal meats.

Calories from fat and protein typically provide a feeling of fullness for longer. The diet may also put your body into the state of ketosis, a process wherein the body burns fat for energy instead of carbohydrates.

- Decreased food sensitivity

Since you are only eating meat, you are also eliminating a range of unhealthy foods from your diet. These are items that are highly processed, high in refined sugar, high in sodium, gluten, and trans-fat. Avoiding these foods may also help prevent inflammation, a common cause for many illnesses.

- Improved digestion

People on a carnivore diet have reported having less distension, bloating, and gas.

- Improved cognitive functions

Diets high in red meat are abundant in vitamins, minerals, and antioxidants that may help with poor concentration, brain fog, depression, and anxiety.

Red meat is rich in iron, zinc, selenium, vitamins B3, B6, and B12. It is a wonderful source of protein, creatine, taurine, and carnosine that are all beneficial for the brain.

Tips for Getting Started

Starting a new diet plan can be very daunting. One useful tip to follow regardless of the type of diet is to figure out why you want to do it. The first few weeks will be the hardest, and knowing why you need to alter your diet and how important it is to your goals will greatly help in keeping you motivated to push through.

Here are more tips to help you get started on the carnivore diet.

- Listen to your body

A carnivore diet can be very restrictive, and some people might be put off with eating only meat. One way to have a successful outcome is to incorporate animal meat into your diet gradually until you can replace all your meals with it. It is okay to include small amounts of vegetables to help with the transition.

- Keep yourself hydrated

Poor hydration and loss of electrolytes result in diarrhea, headache, fatigue, and sleep issues. Remember to keep yourself well hydrated and increase your intake of salt.

- Plan your meals and keep a journal

Meal planning saves you time and money. It will also help you stay within your goals. Keeping a food journal can be very helpful in providing motivation and will help you keep track of the progress you have made.

- Find support

There are many online groups you can join where you can share your experiences, get useful tips, and support while on a carnivore diet. It is a great feeling to know that there are people out there that share your experiences. It is also a terrific avenue to help someone who is also struggling.

Frequently Asked Questions

- Are digestive issues normal?

Yes. It is expected that during the first few weeks on the carnivore diet, you will experience either a decrease or an increase in bowel movement. This is the digestive system's response to the absence of fiber and carbohydrates in your diet. The key is to push through and increase your intake of fluids and electrolytes.

- What should I do when I get food cravings?

One reason behind this is that you might not be eating enough meat. You can either increase your consumption or change up your menu to have variety.

- How much meat should I eat?

There is no rule regarding the right amount of meat one must consume daily. Different people have different lifestyles and needs, that's why the amount will vary. Some may eat up to four servings per day, while others are fine with just one. The best thing to do is to eat whenever you are hungry.

- Is it okay to consume dairy?

Dairy can be consumed but should be limited. If you are wanting to lose weight or have inflammation issues, it is best to eliminate it.

- Can I eat vegetables while on a carnivore diet?

It depends. Some people have no trouble transitioning to an all-meat diet, and that's perfectly fine. Although the carnivore diet only promotes animal products, it is up to you if you want to include some vegetables as long as they are in moderate quantity.

- Is it okay to eat processed meat?

Ideally, no. But if you can't avoid it, make sure that you consume it in moderation. Although it is still meat, processed meat like sausages, hotdogs, ham, salami, and jerky may contain high amounts of fillers, sugar, salt, and preservatives (nitrates). The carnivore diet encourages the consumption of organic, grass-fed, and unprocessed meat to maximize the benefits.

Chapter 2: Overview of the Air Fryer

What is the Air Fryer?

An air fryer is a kitchen appliance that can mimic the taste and texture of fried food without using as much oil. Unlike deep-fried food, air fried dishes are deemed to be healthier. Air fryers are small enough to fit in your kitchen counter-top and can perform other functions such as roast, bake, and broil.

How Does the Air Fryer Work?

Air fryers are closely similar to convection ovens since it uses the same method to cook food. Air fryers have heating elements that are usually positioned at the top of the appliance and convection fans to dissipate the heat. The rapidly circulating hot air cooks the food evenly and gives it an appetizing golden-brown color.

Guidelines for Usage, Care, and Maintenance

It is important to read the user's manual before operating your air fryer. Not only will this guarantee your safety, but will also keep your unit in excellent working condition for longer. Here are a few things to remember when using an air fryer.

- Placement

You might think that finding a spot for your air fryer isn't that important. It is if you want to keep accidents from happening. The air fryer should be located on a flat and level surface that can withstand heat. Place it away from areas that get wet like the sink, and areas that get hot like the gas range or oven. It is also crucial to leave enough space on all sides of your appliance.

- Exercise caution

When using the air fryer, make sure that all parts are in good working condition. Don't use it if you see any damage to the wires and other important components. Use oven mitts to avoid any burns and do not leave it unattended when cooking.

- Cleaning and maintenance

Turn off and unplug the unit after use. Once completely cool to the touch, remove the frying pan together with the basket for washing. Air fryer components are easy to clean, thanks to their nonstick coating. If you encountered food that is hard to remove, simply soak the basket and pan in hot water with some dishwashing soap for a few hours before washing. Wipe the main body with a clean damp cloth to remove any dirt or grease. Keep the air fryer body, wire, and other electrical parts away from any liquids. Conduct deep cleaning whenever necessary.

Air Fryer Cooking Tips

Cooking in an air fryer is easy as most units come with cooking presets. Here are other valuable tips when using your air fryer.

- Preheat your air fryer

Some recipes require preheating. To do this, simply set the timer for two or three minutes. Some air fryers will already have a dedicated button for preheating.

- Do not overload the frying basket

To make sure that the food cooks properly, leave space for the hot air to circulate.

- Don't forget to turn or shake the food

To guarantee even cooking, browning, and crisping, flip or shake the food every five to ten minutes or halfway through the cooking time.

- Add a light coating of oil

Oil helps keep the food from sticking to the frying basket and also gives it a nice golden-brown color and crisp. Lightly brush or spray a coating of oil before putting food and also halfway through the cooking time.

- Check the food from time to time

Although we love the cooking presets that come with air fryers, it is not fool-proof. Make sure that you check for doneness every few minutes to avoid overcooking the food.

Chapter 3: Breakfast Recipes

Maple Breakfast Sausage

Preparation Time: 10 minutes

Cooking Time: 10 minutes

Servings: 6

Ingredients:

- 1 lb. ground turkey
- 1 lb. ground pork
- ½ cup maple syrup
- 1 teaspoon dried sage
- 1 teaspoon dried thyme
- Salt and pepper to taste

Method:

1. Combine all the ingredients in a bowl.
2. Form patties from the mixture.
3. Place them in the air fryer rack.
4. Set it to 400 degrees F.
5. Cook for 5 minutes per side.

Serving Suggestions: Serve with toasted bread.

Preparation & Cooking Tips: Use lean ground pork.

Crispy Bacon

Preparation Time: 5 minutes

Cooking Time: 10 minutes

Servings: 6

Ingredients:

- 1 lb. bacon

Method:

1. Preheat your air fryer to 400 degrees F.
2. Add the bacon slices to your air fryer basket.
3. Cook for 10 minutes, flipping once or twice.

Serving Suggestions: Serve as is or with your favorite condiments.

Preparation & Cooking Tips: Extend cooking time if you want your bacon crispier.

Ham & Egg Cups

Preparation Time: 10 minutes

Cooking Time: 15 minutes

Servings: 6

Ingredients:

- 4 eggs
- 4 tablespoons heavy cream
- ¼ cup cheddar cheese, shredded
- 3 slices ham, diced
- 3 stalks scallions, chopped
- Salt and pepper to taste
- Cooking spray

Method:

1. Beat the eggs in a bowl until frothy.
2. Stir in the rest of the ingredients.
3. Spray your muffin pan with oil.
4. Pour the mixture into the muffin cups.
5. Place the muffin pan in the air fryer.
6. Set it to 300 degrees F.
7. Cook for 10 to 15 minutes or until eggs are set.

Serving Suggestions: Serve with your favorite condiments.

Preparation & Cooking Tips: You can also add chopped mushrooms into the mixture.

Beef & Egg Rolls

Preparation Time: 30 minutes

Cooking Time: 6 minutes

Servings: 12

Ingredients:

- 1 cup scrambled eggs
- 1 lb. ground beef, cooked
- ½ cup cheddar cheese, shredded
- 12 egg roll wrappers
- Cooking spray

Method:

1. In a bowl, mix the eggs, beef and cheese.
2. Place a spoonful of the mixture on top of the egg wrappers.
3. Roll up the wrappers and seal.
4. Air fry at 340 degrees F for 6 minutes, turning once or twice.

Serving Suggestions: Serve with sweet chili sauce.

Preparation & Cooking Tips: You can also add chopped scallions to the mixture.

French Toast Rolls with Sausage

Preparation Time: 10 minutes

Cooking Time: 5 minutes

Servings: 8

Ingredients:

- 8 sausages, cooked
- 8 slices bread
- 2 eggs, beaten
- 1 teaspoon vanilla extract
- ½ cup milk

Method:

1. Add the sausages on top of the bread slices.
2. Roll up the bread.
3. Secure with a toothpick.
4. In a bowl, mix the eggs, vanilla and milk.
5. Dip the rolls in the mixture.
6. Place in the air fryer rack.
7. Air fry at 350 degrees F for 5 minutes.

Serving Suggestions: Sprinkle with ground cinnamon.

Preparation & Cooking Tips: Trim the edges of the bread.

Breakfast Muffin with Bacon & Eggs

Preparation Time: 10 minutes

Cooking Time: 15 minutes

Servings: 6

Ingredients:

- 1 tablespoon olive oil
- 6 slices bacon
- 3 eggs, beaten
- 3 English muffins, split in half

Method:

1. Pour the oil into a pan over medium heat.
2. Add the bacon and cook until crispy.
3. Transfer to a plate lined with paper towel and drain.
4. Add the eggs.
5. Cook while stirring until set.
6. Transfer to a plate.
7. Top the muffins with the egg and bacon.
8. Top with the other muffin slice.
9. Place in the air fryer rack.
10. Air fry at 320 degrees for 3 minutes per side.

Serving Suggestions: Serve with mayo and ketchup.

Preparation & Cooking Tips: You can also add a slice of Provolone cheese to your sandwich.

Bacon Burrito

Preparation Time: 5 minutes

Cooking Time: 5 minutes

Servings: 2

Ingredients:

- 2 eggs, scrambled
- ½ cup cheddar cheese, shredded
- 4 slices bacon, cooked crisp and crumbled
- 2 flour tortillas

Method:

1. Combine eggs, cheese and bacon in a bowl.
2. Top the tortilla with the mixture.
3. Roll up the tortillas.
4. Place the tortillas in the air fryer rack.
5. Air fry at 250 degrees F for 5 minutes.

Serving Suggestions: Serve with hot pepper sauce.

Preparation & Cooking Tips: You can add more bacon if you like.

Sausage & Egg Bites

Preparation Time: 10 minutes

Cooking Time: 10 minutes

Servings: 4

Ingredients:

- 6 eggs
- ¾ cup milk
- 6 sausages, cooked and crumbled
- 1 cup cheddar cheese, shredded
- Cooking spray

Method:

1. Beat the eggs and milk in a bowl.
2. Stir in the crumbled sausages and cheese.
3. Spray your muffin pan with oil.
4. Pour the mixture into the muffin cups.
5. Place the muffin pan in the air fryer.
6. Cook at 320 degrees F for 8 to 10 minutes.

Serving Suggestions: Garnish with chopped scallions.

Preparation & Cooking Tips: If eggs are not fully done after 10 minutes, extend cooking time.

Sausage Patties

Preparation Time: 5 minutes

Cooking Time: 10 minutes

Servings: 8

Ingredients:

- 8 frozen sausage patties

Method:

1. Spread the patties on the air fryer rack.
2. Air fry at 400 degrees F for 10 minutes, flipping once.

Serving Suggestions: Serve with mustard and ketchup.

Breakfast Potatoes with Bacon & Ham

Preparation Time: 15 minutes

Cooking Time: 20 minutes

Servings: 8

Ingredients:

- 1 onion, chopped
- 2 lb. potatoes, sliced into cubes
- 2 slices ham, diced
- 5 slices bacon, diced
- 2 tablespoons olive oil
- 1 teaspoon smoked paprika
- 2 tablespoons dried rosemary
- Salt and pepper to taste

Method:

1. Toss the onion, potatoes, ham and bacon in olive oil.
2. Season with paprika, rosemary, salt and pepper.
3. Add the mixture to the air fryer basket.
4. Cook at 400 degrees F for 15 minutes.
5. Stir and cook for another 5 minutes.

Serving Suggestions: Garnish with dried herbs.

Preparation & Cooking Tips: Use red potatoes for this recipe.

Chapter 4: Beef

Garlic Mustard Steak

Preparation Time: 5 minutes

Cooking Time: 10 minutes

Servings: 2

Ingredients:

- 2 cloves garlic, minced
- 2 sirloin steaks
- 2 tablespoons Dijon-style mustard
- 4 tablespoons vegetable oil
- Salt and pepper to taste

Method:

1. Sprinkle minced garlic on top of the steaks.
2. In a bowl, mix the mustard, oil, salt and pepper.
3. Brush both sides of the steak with the mixture.
4. Marinate for 30 minutes.
5. Add the steaks to the air fryer basket.
6. Cook at 400 degrees F for 4 to 5 minutes per side.

Serving Suggestions: Serve with mashed potatoes and gravy.

Preparation & Cooking Tips: Internal temperature of beef should be 160 degrees F for well done.

Korean Beef Short Ribs

Preparation Time: 5 minutes

Cooking Time: 5 minutes

Servings: 4

Ingredients:

- ½ cup soy sauce
- 1 teaspoon garlic, minced
- ½ cup brown sugar
- ½ teaspoon red pepper flakes
- 1 tablespoon ground ginger
- 2 lb. beef short ribs

Method:

1. Add all the ingredients except beef short ribs in a sealable plastic bag.
2. Shake to mix well.
3. Add the ribs to the plastic bag.
4. Turn to coat evenly.
5. Refrigerate for 1 hour.
6. Place the ribs in the air fryer.
7. Air fry at 400 degrees F for 3 minutes per side.

Serving Suggestions: Garnish with chopped green onions and sesame seeds.

Preparation & Cooking Tips: You can also add salt and pepper to the marinade.

Beef Liver & Onions

Preparation Time: 10 minutes

Cooking Time: 10 minutes

Servings: 2

Ingredients:

- 1 teaspoon onion powder
- 1 teaspoon garlic powder
- 1 teaspoon smoked paprika
- 1 teaspoon dry mustard
- Salt and pepper to taste
- 1 ½ lb. beef liver
- 2 onions, sliced into rings

Method:

1. Mix the onion powder, garlic powder, paprika, mustard, salt and pepper in a bowl.
2. Season calf liver and onion rings with this mixture.
3. Spread the onions in the air fryer basket.
4. Top with the liver.
5. Cook at 370 degrees F for 7 minutes.
6. Transfer the liver to a plate.
7. Cook the onions for 3 more minutes.
8. Top the liver with the onions.

Serving Suggestions: Sprinkle with pepper before serving.

Preparation & Cooking Tips: Use baby calf liver.

Flank Steak with Chimichurri

Preparation Time: 10 minutes

Cooking Time: 12 minutes

Servings: 4

Ingredients:

- 2 lb. flank steak
- 1 tablespoon olive oil
- Salt and pepper to taste

Chimichurri

- ¼ cup olive oil
- 2 tablespoons red wine vinegar
- 1 clove garlic
- ½ onion
- ½ cup cilantro, sliced
- ½ cup parsley, sliced
- ½ teaspoon red pepper flakes
- Salt and pepper to taste

Method:

1. Preheat the air fryer to 400 degrees F for 5 minutes.
2. Brush both sides of steaks with oil.
3. Season with salt and pepper.
4. Air fry for 6 minutes per side.
5. Add the chimichurri ingredients to a food processor.
6. Pulse until chopped and mixed.

7. Serve the steak with the chimichurri.

Serving Suggestions: Serve with grilled corn.

Preparation & Cooking Tips: Let steak sit at room temperature for 30 minutes before seasoning and cooking.

Steak with Chipotle Butter

Preparation Time: 10 minutes

Cooking Time: 15 minutes

Servings: 2

Ingredients:

- 2 rib eye steaks

Dry rub

- 1 teaspoon cocoa powder
- 1 ½ teaspoon chili powder
- ½ teaspoon brown sugar
- Salt and pepper to taste

Butter sauce

- 1 tablespoon chipotle chili
- ¼ cup butter, softened
- 1 teaspoon brown sugar
- Salt to taste

Method:

1. Combine the dry rub ingredients in a bowl.
2. Rub both sides of steaks with this mixture.
3. Place in the air fryer rack.
4. Air fry at 400 degrees F for 7 minutes.
5. Flip and cook for another 5 minutes.
6. Mix the butter sauce ingredients.

7. Top the steaks with the butter sauce.

Serving Suggestions: Let steak rest for 10 minutes before serving.

Preparation & Cooking Tips: Marinate steaks for 30 minutes before air frying.

Cheese Stuffed Meatloaf

Preparation Time: 5 minutes

Cooking Time: 15 minutes

Servings: 4

Ingredients:

- 2 lb. ground beef
- 1 teaspoon dried Italian seasoning
- Salt and pepper to taste
- ½ cup mozzarella cheese
- 1 cup marinara sauce

Method:

1. Season the beef with the Italian herbs, salt and pepper.
2. Mix well.
3. Press beef into a loaf pan.
4. Insert the cheese in the middle part of the meatloaf.
5. Brush the top with the marinara sauce.
6. Place the meatloaf inside the air fryer.
7. Set it to 340 degrees F.
8. Cook for 10 to 15 minutes.

Serving Suggestions: Top with caramelized onions.

Preparation & Cooking Tips: You can also use 1 lb. ground beef and 1 lb. ground turkey for this recipe.

Carne Asada

Preparation Time: 1 hour and 10 minutes

Cooking Time: 15 minutes

Servings: 6

Ingredients:

- 1 ½ lb. flank steak
- Cooking spray

Marinade

- ¼ cup olive oil
- ¼ cup lime juice
- 4 cloves garlic, minced
- ½ cup cilantro, chopped
- 1 teaspoon chili powder
- 1 teaspoon cumin powder
- Salt and pepper to taste

Method:

1. Mix the marinade ingredients in a bowl.
2. Add steak to the marinade.
3. Cover the bowl.
4. Refrigerate for 1 hour.
5. Spray the air fryer basket with oil.
6. Add the steak to the basket.
7. Cook at 400 degrees F for 7 minutes per side.

Serving Suggestions: Serve with choice side dish.

Preparation & Cooking Tips: Internal temperature should be 145 degrees F.

Country-Style Steak

Preparation Time: 10 minutes

Cooking Time: 10 minutes

Servings: 4

Ingredients:

- 1 egg, beaten
- ¼ cup milk
- 1 cup flour
- Salt and pepper to taste
- 4 steaks
- Cooking spray

Method:

1. Mix the egg and milk in a bowl.
2. In another bowl, combine flour, salt and pepper.
3. Dip the steaks in egg mixture.
4. Dredge with flour.
5. Spray with oil.
6. Add the steaks to the air fryer basket.
7. Cook at 400 degrees F for 5 minutes per side.

Serving Suggestions: Serve with gravy.

Preparation & Cooking Tips: You can also use beef tenderloin for this recipe.

Rib Eye Steak with Blue Cheese Sauce

Preparation Time: 10 minutes

Cooking Time: 15 minutes

Servings: 2

Ingredients:

- 1/8 cup olive oil
- 2 teaspoons steak seasoning
- 2 teaspoon Worcestershire sauce
- ¼ cup soy sauce
- 2 rib eye steaks

Blue cheese sauce

- ½ cup butter, softened
- ½ cup blue cheese, crumbled
- 1 tablespoon parsley, diced

Method:

1. Mix olive oil, steak seasoning, Worcestershire sauce and soy sauce in a bowl.
2. Add the steaks.
3. Cover and marinate for 3 hours.
4. Place in the air fryer basket.
5. Cook at 400 degrees F for 7 minutes per side.
6. Mix the blue cheese sauce ingredients.
7. Pour the sauce over the steaks and serve.

Serving Suggestions: Serve with side dish of choice.

Preparation & Cooking Tips: Internal temperature should be 160 degrees F for well-done, and 150 degrees F for medium well.

Garlic Butter Steak

Preparation Time: 10 minutes

Cooking Time: 10 minutes

Servings: 2

Ingredients:

Garlic butter

- 2 tablespoons butter, softened
- 1 teaspoon garlic, minced
- 1 teaspoon parsley, chopped
- 1 teaspoon soy sauce

Steak

- 2 rib eye steaks
- Salt and pepper to taste

Method:

1. Mix the garlic butter ingredients in a bowl.
2. Sprinkle both sides of steaks with salt and pepper.
3. Air fry at 400 degrees F for 3 minutes per side.
4. Top with the garlic butter and serve.

Serving Suggestions: Serve with grilled veggies.

Preparation & Cooking Tips: You can also use sirloin or T-bone steak for this recipe.

Chapter 5: Pork

Pork Teriyaki

Preparation Time: 10 minutes

Cooking Time: 20 minutes

Servings: 4

Ingredients:

- 1 tablespoon vegetable oil
- 2 tablespoons soy sauce
- 1 tablespoon rice vinegar
- 1 tablespoon dry sherry
- 1 tablespoon brown sugar
- 1 teaspoon ginger, grated
- 2 cloves garlic, minced
- Salt and pepper to taste
- 1 lb. pork tenderloin, sliced into strips

Method:

1. Combine all ingredients for the sauce.
2. Add the pork to the sauce.
3. Cover and marinate for 5 hours.
4. Preheat your air fryer to 400 degrees F.
5. Cook the pork in the air fryer for 25 minutes, stirring once or twice.

Serving Suggestions: Sprinkle with white sesame seeds.

Preparation & Cooking Tips: You can also use pork chop strips for this recipe but extend cooking time to 30 minutes.

Kielbasa

Preparation Time: 10 minutes

Cooking Time: 10 minutes

Servings: 4

Ingredients:

- 1 pack kielbasa

Method:

1. Preheat your air fryer to 350 degrees F.
2. Add the kielbasa to your air fryer rack.
3. Cook for 4 minutes per side.

Serving Suggestions: Serve with your favorite condiments.

Preparation & Cooking Tips: Let kielbasa rest for 5 minutes before slicing and serving.

Honey Glazed Ham

Preparation Time: 10 minutes

Cooking Time: 40 minutes

Servings: 6

Ingredients:

- 1 cup brown sugar
- 1 cup honey
- 2 lb. ham

Method:

1. Add sugar and honey to a pan over medium heat.
2. Simmer while stirring until sugar has been dissolved.
3. Add the ham to a small baking pan.
4. Pour half of the honey mixture on top.
5. Place the pan in the air fryer.
6. Air fry at 310 degrees F for 20 minutes.
7. Pour the remaining honey mixture.
8. Cook for another 20 minutes.

Serving Suggestions: Let rest before slicing and serving.

Preparation & Cooking Tips: You can also use maple syrup in place of honey.

Barbecue Pork

Preparation Time: 20 minutes

Cooking Time: 10 minutes

Servings: 2

Ingredients:

- 1 lb. pork tenderloin, sliced

Barbecue sauce

- 2/3 cup ketchup
- ½ cup cider vinegar
- ¼ cup brown sugar
- 1 teaspoon paprika
- 1 teaspoon ground cumin
- Salt and pepper to taste

Method:

1. Add all the sauce ingredients to a pan over medium heat.
2. Simmer for 7 minutes.
3. Transfer to a bowl and let cool.
4. Stir in the pork tenderloin.
5. Cover and marinate for 4 hours.
6. Place the pork in the air fryer basket.
7. Cook at 400 degrees F for 10 minutes.

Serving Suggestions: Serve with grilled corn.

Preparation & Cooking Tips: You can also use pre-made barbecue sauce.

Apricot Pork Chops

Preparation Time: 10 minutes

Cooking Time: 20 minutes

Servings: 2

Ingredients:

- 2 pork chops
- Salt and pepper to taste
- Cooking spray
- 1 tablespoon olive oil
- 1 clove garlic, minced
- ½ cup apricot jam
- 1 teaspoon soy sauce
- ¼ cup water

Method:

1. Sprinkle both sides of pork chops with salt and pepper.
2. Spray your air fryer basket with oil.
3. Add the pork chops to the air fryer basket.
4. Cook at 320 degrees F for 5 minutes.
5. Add the olive oil to a pan over medium heat.
6. Cook the garlic for 30 seconds, stirring frequently.
7. Stir in the rest of the ingredients.
8. Bring to a boil.
9. Reduce heat and simmer for 10 minutes.
10. Dip the pork chops in the apricot sauce and serve.

Serving Suggestions: Garnish with fresh parsley.

Preparation & Cooking Tips: Flatten the pork with a meat mallet before cooking.

Breaded Pork Chops

Preparation Time: 5 minutes

Cooking Time: 15 minutes

Servings: 4

Ingredients:

- 4 pork chops
- 1 egg, beaten
- 1 cup breadcrumbs
- 2/3 cups cornflake crumbs
- 2 teaspoons sweet paprika
- 1 teaspoon onion powder
- 1 teaspoon garlic powder
- 1 teaspoon chili powder
- Salt and pepper to taste
- Cooking spray

Method:

1. Sprinkle both sides of pork chops with salt and pepper.
2. Dip pork chops in eggs.
3. In a bowl, mix the remaining ingredients.
4. Dredge the pork chops with this mixture.
5. Spray your air fryer basket with oil.
6. Air fry the pork chops for 6 to 7 minutes per side.

Serving Suggestions: Serve with gravy.

Preparation & Cooking Tips: Internal temperature should be 145 degrees F.

Crispy Pork Belly

Preparation Time: 10 minutes

Cooking Time: 30 minutes

Servings: 4

Ingredients:

- 1 lb. pork belly
- 2 tablespoons olive oil
- Salt to taste

Method:

1. Coat pork belly with oil.
2. Sprinkle with salt.
3. Place in the air fryer basket.
4. Cook at 350 degrees F for 10 minutes.
5. Increase temperature to 400 degrees F.
6. Cook for another 10 minutes.

Serving Suggestions: Serve with garlic vinegar dip.

Preparation & Cooking Tips: Sprinkle with minced garlic before seasoning with salt.

Honey Garlic Pork Chops

Preparation Time: 10 minutes

Cooking Time: 20 minutes

Servings: 4

Ingredients:

- 4 pork chops
- Salt and pepper to taste
- 4 tablespoons olive oil
- 4 cloves garlic, minced
- 2 tablespoons sweet chili sauce
- 4 tablespoons lemon juice
- ½ cup honey

Method:

1. Sprinkle both sides of pork chops with salt and pepper.
2. Add these to the air fryer basket.
3. Cook at 400 degrees F for 7 minutes per side.
4. In a pan over medium heat, add olive oil and cook garlic for 1 minute.
5. Stir in the rest of the ingredients.
6. Simmer until the sauce has thickened.
7. Pour the sauce over the pork chops and serve.

Serving Suggestions: Garnish with lemon wedges.

Preparation & Cooking Tips: Use bone-in pork chops.

Blackened Pork Chops

Preparation Time: 5 minutes

Cooking Time: 15 minutes

Servings: 4

Ingredients:

- 1 lb. pork chop

Dry rub

- 1 teaspoon garlic powder
- 1 teaspoon chili powder
- 1 teaspoon paprika
- 1 teaspoon dried thyme
- 1 teaspoon cayenne pepper
- 1 teaspoon brown sugar
- Salt and pepper to taste

Method:

1. Mix the dry rub ingredients in a bowl.
2. Rub mixture on both sides of pork chops.
3. Add to the air fryer basket.
4. Cook at 360 degrees F for 7 minutes per side.

Serving Suggestions: Garnish with cucumber rounds.

Preparation & Cooking Tips: Use pork chops that are 1-inch thick.

Parmesan Pork with Herbs

Preparation Time: 10 minutes

Cooking Time: 16 minutes

Servings: 4

Ingredients:

- 4 pork chops
- Salt and pepper to taste
- ½ cup all-purpose flour
- 2 eggs, beaten
- ¼ cup Parmesan Cheese, grated
- ¼ cup breadcrumbs
- 1 teaspoon sugar
- ½ teaspoon basil
- ½ teaspoon garlic powder
- ½ teaspoon thyme
- ½ teaspoon oregano
- Cooking spray

Method:

1. Season both sides of pork chops with salt and pepper.
2. Cover with flour and dip in egg.
3. In a bowl, mix the rest of the ingredients.
4. Dredge pork with this mixture.
5. Spray pork with oil.
6. Place in the air fryer basket.
7. Cook at 360 degrees F for 8 minutes.

8. Flip and spray with oil.
9. Cook for another 8 minutes.

Serving Suggestions: Serve with marinara dip.

Preparation & Cooking Tips: Use boneless pork chops.

Chapter 6: Lamb

Garlic & Rosemary Lamb Chops

Preparation Time: 10 minutes

Cooking Time: 6 minutes

Servings: 4

Ingredients:

- 2 tablespoons olive oil
- 2 tablespoons lemon juice
- 1 teaspoon lemon zest
- 4 teaspoons garlic, minced
- 1 tablespoon rosemary, chopped
- Salt and pepper to taste
- 1 lb. lamb chops

Method:

1. Combine all ingredients except lamb in a bowl.
2. Mix well.
3. Add the lamb chops to the marinade.
4. Cover and marinate for 1 hour.
5. Place in the air fryer basket.
6. Air fry at 400 degrees F for 3 minutes per side.

Serving Suggestions: Sprinkle with pepper before serving.

Preparation & Cooking Tips: Let lamb chops come to room temperature for 30 minutes before seasoning.

Roast Lamb

Preparation Time: 10 minutes

Cooking Time: 20 minutes

Servings: 4

Ingredients:

- 10 oz. lamb leg roast, butterflied
- 1 tablespoon olive oil
- 1 teaspoon dried rosemary
- 1 teaspoon dried thyme
- Pepper to taste

Method:

1. Preheat your air fryer to 360 degrees F.
2. In a bowl, mix the olive oil and herbs.
3. Rub mixture on all sides of lamb.
4. Place it in the air fryer basket.
5. Cook for 15 minutes.
6. Turn and cook for another 5 minutes.

Serving Suggestions: Let rest for 10 minutes before slicing.

Preparation & Cooking Tips: Slice against the grain.

Lamb with Lemon & Cumin

Preparation Time: 20 minutes
Cooking Time: 30 minutes
Servings: 4

Ingredients:

- 1 rack of lamb
- Salt and pepper to taste
- 2 cloves garlic, minced
- 1 cup breadcrumbs
- 1 teaspoon ground cumin
- 1 teaspoon cumin seeds
- 1 teaspoon olive oil
- ½ tablespoon lemon zest
- 2 eggs, beaten

Method:

1. Preheat your air fryer to 250 degrees F.
2. Season all sides of lamb with salt and pepper.
3. Mix the remaining ingredients except eggs in a bowl.
4. Dip the lamb in eggs.
5. Dredge with breadcrumb mixture.
6. Add the lamb to the air fryer basket.
7. Cook for 25 minutes.
8. Increase temperature to 400 degrees F.
9. Cook for another 5 minutes.

Serving Suggestions: Cover with foil for 5 minutes before serving.

Preparation & Cooking Tips: It's a good idea to French cut the lamb before preparing.

Lamb Chops with Herb Butter

Preparation Time: 5 minutes

Cooking Time: 5 minutes

Servings: 4

Ingredients:

- 8 lamb chops
- 2 tablespoons butter, softened
- 2 teaspoon rosemary, chopped

Method:

1. Preheat your air fryer to 400 degrees F.
2. Place the lamb chops in the air fryer basket.
3. Cook the lamb chops for 5 minutes.
4. Mix the butter and rosemary.
5. Top the lamb chops with the herbed butter and serve.

Serving Suggestions: Garnish with fresh rosemary leaves.

Preparation & Cooking Tips: You can also use dried rosemary if fresh herbs are not available.

Greek Lamb Chops

Preparation Time: 5 minutes

Cooking Time: 10 minutes

Servings: 4

Ingredients:

- ¼ cup olive oil
- ¼ cup lemon juice
- 2 teaspoon dried oregano
- 2 cloves garlic, minced
- Salt and pepper to taste
- 2 lb. lamb chops

Method:

1. Combine the olive oil, lemon juice, oregano, garlic, salt and pepper in a bowl.
2. Stir in the lamb chops.
3. Add the lamb chops to the air fryer basket.
4. Cook at 400 degrees F for 5 minutes per side.

Serving Suggestions: Serve with feta cheese and olives.

Preparation & Cooking Tips: Use freshly squeezed lemon juice.

Lamb Chops with Horseradish Sauce

Preparation Time: 10 minutes

Cooking Time: 13 minutes

Servings: 2

Ingredients:

Lamb chops

- 4 lamb chops
- 2 tablespoons vegetable oil
- 1 clove garlic, minced
- Salt and pepper to taste

Horseradish cream sauce

- 1 ½ tablespoons horseradish
- ½ cup mayonnaise
- 2 teaspoons sugar

Method:

1. Coat lamb chops with oil.
2. Sprinkle with garlic, salt and pepper.
3. Marinate for 30 minutes.
4. Mix the sauce ingredients in a bowl.
5. Take half of the sauce.
6. Spread on both sides of the lamb.
7. Cook in the air fryer at 325 degrees F for 5 minutes per side.
8. Increase temperature to 400 degrees F.
9. Cook for another 3 minutes.

Serving Suggestions: Serve with the remaining sauce.

Preparation & Cooking Tips: Use light mayonnaise.

Mint Lamb

Preparation Time: 10 minutes

Cooking Time: 10 minutes

Servings: 4

Ingredients:

- 4 lamb chops
- 1 tablespoon olive oil
- 2 tablespoons mint leaves, chopped
- Salt and pepper to taste

Method:

1. Coat the lamb chops with the olive oil.
2. Sprinkle with mint leaves, salt and pepper.
3. Add to the air fryer.
4. Air fry at 400 degrees F for 5 minutes per side.

Serving Suggestions: Garnish with mint leaves.

Preparation & Cooking Tips: You can also sprinkle toasted hazelnuts on top.

Herbed Rack of Lamb

Preparation Time: 5 minutes

Cooking Time: 15 minutes

Servings: 4

Ingredients:

- 1 rack of lamb
- 4 tablespoons olive oil
- 2 teaspoons garlic, minced
- 1 tablespoon dried thyme
- 2 tablespoons dried rosemary
- Salt and pepper to taste

Method:

1. In a bowl, mix the olive oil, garlic and herbs.
2. Rub mixture on all sides of lamb.
3. Sprinkle with salt and pepper.
4. Place in the air fryer.
5. Cook at 360 degrees F for 10 minutes.
6. Turn and cook for another 5 minutes.

Serving Suggestions: Serve with mustard.

Preparation & Cooking Tips: Internal temperature should be 165 degrees F.

Lamb with Lemon & Coriander

Preparation Time: 1 hour and 10 minutes

Cooking Time: 10 minutes

Servings: 4

Ingredients:

- 1 teaspoon of coriander
- 1 teaspoon rosemary
- 1 teaspoon oregano
- 1 teaspoon thyme
- Salt to taste
- 2 tablespoons olive oil
- 2 tablespoons lemon juice
- 4 lamb chops

Method:

1. Add all the ingredients except lamb chops in a bowl.
2. Mix well.
3. Stir in the lamb chops.
4. Cover and refrigerate for 1 hour.
5. Transfer lamb chops to the air fryer.
6. Cook at 390 degrees F for 3 minutes.
7. Flip and cook for another 4 minutes.

Serving Suggestions: Garnish with fresh herbs.

Preparation & Cooking Tips: If you want your lamb chops well done, cook for another 3 minutes.

Italian Lamb Chops

Preparation Time: 3 hours and 10 minutes

Cooking Time: 25 minutes

Servings: 8

Ingredients:

- 1 teaspoon Italian spice blend
- 2 teaspoons olive oil
- 2 teaspoons mustard
- 1 teaspoon soy sauce
- 1 teaspoon garlic, minced
- 1 teaspoon cayenne pepper
- 1 teaspoon cumin powder
- Salt to taste
- 8 lamb chops

Method:

1. Combine all the ingredients except lamb chops in a sealable plastic bag.
2. Seal and shake to combine.
3. Add the lamb to the plastic bag.
4. Refrigerate for 3 hours.
5. Transfer to the air fryer rack.
6. Air fry at 350 degrees F for 17 minutes.
7. Flip and cook for another 5 to 6 minutes.

Serving Suggestions: Sprinkle with a little bit more cumin and salt.

Preparation & Cooking Tips: Use Dijon style mustard for this recipe.

Chapter 7: Fish & Seafood

Honey Lemon Salmon

Preparation Time: 10 minutes

Cooking Time: 10 minutes

Servings: 2

Ingredients:

- 2 salmon fillets
- Salt and pepper to taste
- 4 tablespoons honey
- ½ cup butter, melted
- 3 tablespoons lemon juice

Method:

1. Season salmon with salt and pepper.
2. In a bowl, mix honey, butter and lemon juice.
3. Brush both sides with this mixture.
4. Add the fish to the air fryer basket.
5. Air fry at 390 degrees F for 7 to 10 minutes or until flaky.

Serving Suggestions: Garnish with lemon wedges.

Preparation & Cooking Tips: You can also use white fish fillet for this recipe.

Salmon with Mustard Sauce

Preparation Time: 10 minutes

Cooking Time: 8 minutes

Servings: 2

Ingredients:

- 2 salmon fillets
- 1 tablespoon Dijon mustard
- 2 tablespoons olive oil
- 1 tablespoon garlic, minced
- ½ teaspoon ground thyme
- 2 tablespoons lemon juice
- Salt and pepper to taste

Method:

1. Place the salmon fillets on a baking sheet.
2. Mix the remaining ingredients in a bowl.
3. Spread half of the mustard mixture on both sides of the salmon.
4. Place the salmon in the air fryer rack.
5. Set it to 400 degrees F.
6. Cook for 5 minutes.
7. Spread the remaining mixture on top side of the salmon.
8. Cook for another 3 minutes.

Serving Suggestions: Sprinkle with pepper before serving.

Preparation & Cooking Tips: You can swap minced garlic with garlic powder.

Spicy Shrimp

Preparation Time: 10 minutes

Cooking Time: 8 minutes

Servings: 6

Ingredients:

- 2 lb. shrimp, peeled and deveined
- 1 teaspoon garlic powder
- 1 teaspoon ground cumin
- 1 teaspoon smoked paprika
- 1 teaspoon chili powder
- 1 teaspoon hot pepper sauce
- 1 teaspoon sugar
- 1 tablespoon lemon juice
- 2 tablespoons Worcestershire sauce
- Salt and pepper to taste

Method:

1. Add the shrimp to a bowl.
2. In another bowl, mix the spices.
3. Coat shrimp with the spice mixture.
4. Place shrimp in the air fryer rack.
5. Cook at 400 degrees F for 4 minutes.
6. Flip and cook for another 4 minutes.

Serving Suggestions: Garnish with chopped scallions.

Preparation & Cooking Tips: You can also use frozen shrimp for this recipe but add 2 to 3 minutes to cooking time.

Shrimp Bang Bang

Preparation Time: 20 minutes

Cooking Time: 10 minutes

Servings: 8

Ingredients:

- 1 lb. shrimp, peeled and deveined
- ¼ cup flour
- 2 eggs, beaten
- 2 cups breadcrumbs
- Cooking spray

Sauce

- ¼ cup mayonnaise
- 2 teaspoons hot pepper sauce
- 2 tablespoons sweet chili sauce
- 1 teaspoon rice vinegar
- 1 tablespoon honey

Method:

1. Coat shrimp with flour.
2. Dip in eggs.
3. Dredge with breadcrumbs.
4. Spray with oil.
5. Air fry at 350 degrees F for 10 minutes, turning once.
6. In a bowl, mix the sauce ingredients.
7. Dip shrimp in the sauce before serving.

Serving Suggestions: Sprinkle chopped parsley on top of shrimp.

Preparation & Cooking Tips: Use jumbo shrimp for this recipe if available.

Crab Cakes

Preparation Time: 1 hour and 10 minutes

Cooking Time: 15 minutes

Servings: 4

Ingredients:

- 1 cup crab meat
- 1 onion, diced
- 2 tablespoons mayonnaise
- ½ teaspoon Dijon mustard
- 1 egg, beaten
- 1 teaspoon Old Bay seasoning
- 1 teaspoon Worcestershire sauce
- 2 tablespoons fresh parsley, chopped
- ½ cup breadcrumbs
- Salt to taste

Method:

1. Mix all the ingredients in a bowl.
2. Form patties from the mixture.
3. Cover patties with plastic and refrigerate for 1 hour.
4. Transfer to the air fryer basket.
5. Cook at 350 degrees F for 15 minutes, flipping once halfway through the cooking.

Serving Suggestions: Garnish with lemon slices.

Preparation & Cooking Tips: You can also add chopped mushrooms into the mixture.

Blackened Shrimp

Preparation Time: 10 minutes

Cooking Time: 8 minutes

Servings: 4

Ingredients:

- 1 lb. shrimp
- 2 tablespoons olive oil
- 1 tablespoon garlic, minced
- 2 teaspoons paprika
- 1 teaspoon onion powder
- ½ teaspoon dried oregano
- ½ teaspoon dried thyme
- ¼ teaspoon cayenne pepper
- Salt and pepper to taste

Method:

1. Brush both sides of shrimp with oil.
2. In a bowl, mix the rest of the ingredients.
3. Sprinkle shrimp with spice mixture.
4. Place shrimp in the air fryer basket.
5. Cook at 400 degrees F for 3 to 4 minutes per side.

Serving Suggestions: Garnish with cucumber rounds or shredded carrots.

Preparation & Cooking Tips: Arrange shrimp in the air fryer basket in a single layer.

Herbed Tilapia

Preparation Time: 10 minutes

Cooking Time: 8 minutes

Servings: 4

Ingredients:

- 1 teaspoon lemon juice
- 1 teaspoon garlic powder
- 1 teaspoon dried oregano
- Salt to taste
- 4 tilapia fillets
- Cooking spray

Method:

1. Brush both sides of tilapia with lemon juice.
2. Sprinkle with garlic powder, oregano and salt.
3. Spray with oil.
4. Cook at the air fryer at 400 degrees F for 8 minutes, flipping once.

Serving Suggestions: Sprinkle with pepper before serving.

Preparation & Cooking Tips: Use olive oil cooking spray.

Salmon Patties

Preparation Time: 5 minutes

Cooking Time: 10 minutes

Servings: 4

Ingredients:

- ¼ cup onion, chopped
- 2 cups canned salmon flakes
- 1 egg, beaten
- 1 teaspoon dill weed
- ½ cup breadcrumbs

Method:

1. Start by draining the fish.
2. Combine all the ingredients in a bowl.
3. Form patties from the mixture.
4. Add the patties to the air fryer basket.
5. Cook at 370 degrees F for 5 minutes per side.

Serving Suggestions: Serve with burger buns or rice.

Preparation & Cooking Tips: Drain the salmon completely before preparing.

Grilled Swordfish

Preparation Time: 5 minutes

Cooking Time: 10 minutes

Servings: 4

Ingredients:

- 4 swordfish steaks
- Salt and pepper to taste

Salsa

- 2 cups mango, chopped
- 1 onion, chopped
- ½ cup cilantro, chopped
- 2 tablespoons lime juice

Method:

1. Sprinkle both sides of swordfish with salt and pepper.
2. Air fry at 400 degrees F for 5 minutes per side.
3. Mix the salsa ingredients in a bowl.
4. Top the fish with the salsa before serving.

Serving Suggestions: Sprinkle with some more chopped cilantro on top.

Preparation & Cooking Tips: You can also make the salsa with cucumbers and tomatoes instead of mango.

Shrimp Scampi

Preparation Time: 5 minutes

Cooking Time: 10 minutes

Servings: 4

Ingredients:

- 2 tablespoons olive oil
- 4 tablespoons butter
- 4 cloves garlic, minced
- Salt and pepper to taste
- 1 lb. shrimp, peeled and deveined

Method:

1. Combine oil, butter, garlic, salt and pepper in a bowl.
2. Coat shrimp evenly with this mixture.
3. Cook at 400 degrees F for 5 minutes.
4. Turn and cook for another 5 minutes.

Serving Suggestions: Garnish with chopped parsley.

Preparation & Cooking Tips: If you will use frozen peeled shrimp, add 3 more minutes to cooking time.

Chapter 8: Snack Recipes

Bacon Burger

Preparation Time: 10 minutes

Cooking Time: 16 minutes

Servings: 4

Ingredients:

- 1 ½ lb. ground beef
- ½ cup onion, chopped
- 1 teaspoon Worcestershire sauce
- 1 teaspoon soy sauce
- 1 teaspoon garlic powder
- 1 teaspoon dried parsley
- 4 slices bacon, cooked crisp
- 4 burger buns

Method:

1. Preheat your air fryer to 400 degrees F.
2. In a bowl, mix all the ingredients except bacon and buns.
3. Form patties from the mixture.
4. Add patties to the air fryer basket.
5. Cook for 8 minutes per side.
6. Add burgers to the burger buns.
7. Top with the bacon slices.

Serving Suggestions: Serve with your favorite condiments.

Preparation & Cooking Tips: You can also add cheese slice to your burger.

Sloppy Joe Taco Bake

Preparation Time: 10 minutes

Cooking Time: 15 minutes

Servings: 6

Ingredients:

- 1 lb. ground beef
- 1 package sloppy Joe mix, prepared according to directions
- 2 cans crescent dough sheets
- 2 cups cheddar cheese, shredded

Method:

1. Add the ground beef to a pan over medium heat.
2. Cook until browned.
3. Spread the sloppy Joe mixture on top of the ground beef.
4. Let it heat up for 5 minutes.
5. Spray a small baking pan with oil.
6. Spread half of dough sheets onto the baking pan.
7. Add the beef mixture on top.
8. Sprinkle cheese on top.
9. Top with remaining dough sheet.
10. Air fry at 350 degrees F for 12 minutes.

Serving Suggestions: Let cool before slicing and serving.

Preparation & Cooking Tips: You can also use mozzarella cheese instead of cheddar.

Meatball Sandwich

Preparation Time: 5 minutes

Cooking Time: 10 minutes

Servings: 6

Ingredients:

- 1 pack frozen meatballs
- 16 oz. marinara sauce
- 6 sub rolls

Method:

1. Add meatballs to the air fryer basket.
2. Cook at 350 degrees F for 5 minutes.
3. Pour the sauce into a pan over medium heat.
4. Simmer for 5 minutes.
5. Add the meatballs inside the sub rolls.
6. Pour the sauce over the meatballs.

Serving Suggestions: You can also add lettuce leaves to your sandwich.

Preparation & Cooking Tips: You can also add Provolone cheese slices to your sandwich.

Reuben Sandwich

Preparation Time: 5 minutes

Cooking Time: 10 minutes

Servings: 4

Ingredients:

- ¼ cup thousand island dressing
- 8 slices rye bread
- 1 lb. corned beef, sliced
- 12 oz. sauerkraut, drained
- 4 slices Swiss cheese
- Cooking spray

Method:

1. Spread dressing on top of the rye bread slices.
2. Top with the corned beef, sauerkraut and cheese.
3. Add the other bread slice on top.
4. Air fry at 390 degrees for 4 minutes per side.

Preparation & Cooking Tips: If rye bread is not available, any bread will do.

Mojo Pork Taco

Preparation Time: 10 minutes

Cooking Time: 5 minutes

Servings: 4

Ingredients:

- 1 lb. ground pork
- 2 tablespoons vinegar
- 1 tablespoon orange juice
- 1 tablespoon lime juice
- 1 teaspoon ground cumin
- 1 teaspoon dried oregano
- 1 teaspoon garlic powder
- 1 teaspoon sugar

Method:

1. Add the ground pork to the air fryer.
2. Cook at 400 degrees F for 5 minutes.
3. Transfer the ground pork to a bowl.
4. Stir in the vinegar, juice, herbs, spices and sugar.
5. Mix well.
6. Top the tortillas with the ground pork mixture.

Serving Suggestions: Serve with sour cream, salsa and chopped cilantro.

Preparation & Cooking Tips: Use freshly squeezed lime juice and orange juice.

Prosciutto & Gouda Sandwich

Preparation Time: 5 minutes

Cooking Time: 5 minutes

Servings: 2

Ingredients:

- 6 tablespoons berry jam
- 2 ciabatta rolls
- 6 slices prosciutto
- 4 slices Gouda cheese
- 1 cup arugula

Method:

1. Spread jam on ciabatta rolls.
2. Top with prosciutto, cheese and arugula.
3. Air fry at 350 degrees F for 2 minutes.

Serving Suggestions: Serve with additional berry jam.

Preparation & Cooking Tips: You can also use other types of bread.

Hawaiian Pork Barbecue Tacos

Preparation Time: 15 minutes

Cooking Time: 10 minutes

Servings: 4

Ingredients:

- 1 lb. ground pork
- 1 jalapeno pepper, sliced into strips
- ½ cup pineapple, sliced
- ½ cup barbecue sauce
- 4 flour tortillas
- ¼ cup onions, diced
- ¼ cup cashews, diced
- ¼ cup cilantro, chopped

Method:

1. Mix the ground pepper, jalapeno and pineapples in a bowl.
2. Transfer mixture to the air fryer basket.
3. Cook at 350 degrees F for 5 minutes.
4. Stir and cook for another 5 minutes.
5. Transfer to a plate.
6. Stir in the barbecue sauce.
7. Top tortillas with the mixture.
8. Sprinkle onions, cashews and cilantro.
9. Fold and serve.

Serving Suggestions: Serve with sour cream and hot pepper sauce.

Preparation & Cooking Tips: You can also use corn tortillas for this recipe.

Cheesy Crab Muffin Melt

Preparation Time: 5 minutes

Cooking Time: 5 minutes

Servings: 4

Ingredients:

- 6 oz. crab meat
- 2 tablespoons onions, diced
- ¼ cup celery, chopped
- ¼ cup mayonnaise
- Salt and pepper to taste
- 4 English muffins
- ¼ cheddar cheese, shredded

Method:

1. Combine crab meat, onions, celery, mayo, salt and pepper.
2. Mix well.
3. Top the muffins with the crab mixture.
4. Sprinkle cheese on top.
5. Transfer these to the air fryer rack.
6. Air fry at 300 degrees F for 5 minutes.

Serving Suggestions: Garnish with chopped scallions.

Preparation & Cooking Tips: Add a teaspoon of Tabasco sauce to the mixture to make the crab meat spicy.

Pepperoni Pizza

Preparation Time: 10 minutes

Cooking Time: 15 minutes

Servings: 6

Ingredients:

- Cooking spray
- 1 frozen pizza crust
- 8 oz. pizza sauce
- 1 teaspoon dried oregano
- 2 cups mozzarella cheese, shredded
- 1 pack pepperoni slices

Method:

1. Spray the air fryer basket with oil.
2. Spread the pizza sauce on top of the pizza crust.
3. Sprinkle with the oregano and cheese.
4. Top with the pepperoni slices.
5. Air fry at 275 degrees F for 15 minutes.

Serving Suggestions: Let cool before slicing and serving.

Preparation & Cooking Tips: If crust is not yet golden after 15 minutes, cook for 3 to 5 minutes more.

Grilled Bacon & Apple Sandwich

Preparation Time: 5 minutes

Cooking Time: 10 minutes

Servings: 1

Ingredients:

- 2 slices bread
- 2 teaspoons mayonnaise
- 4 slices cheddar cheese
- 2 slices bacon, cooked crisp
- ½ apple, sliced thinly

Method:

1. Preheat your air fryer to 350 degrees F.
2. Spread mayo on both sides of bread.
3. Top one bread slice with cheese, bacon and apple.
4. Place the other bread slice on top.
5. Air fry to 3 minutes per side.

Serving Suggestions: Serve with your favorite condiments.

Preparation & Cooking Tips: Use whole wheat bread.

Chapter 9: Appetizer Recipes

Sausage Rolls

Preparation Time: 5 minutes

Cooking Time: 10 minutes

Servings: 6

Ingredients:

- 1 pack refrigerated biscuits
- 1 pack sausages

Method:

1. Roll out the biscuits.
2. Wrap biscuits around the sausages.
3. Add the rolls to your air fryer tray.
4. Cook at 330 degrees F for 10 minutes.

Serving Suggestions: Serve with mayo and ketchup.

Preparation & Cooking Tips: You can also use hotdogs for this recipe.

Pork & Veggie Rolls

Preparation Time: 20 minutes

Cooking Time: 10 minutes

Servings: 6

Ingredients:

- 1 pack egg roll wrappers
- 1 cup ground pork, cooked
- 1 carrot, sliced into strips
- 1 cup cabbage, shredded
- Cooking spray

Method:

1. Top the wrappers with ground pork, carrot and cabbage.
2. Roll up and seal edges with water.
3. Spray rolls with oil.
4. Place these in the air fryer basket.
5. Cook at 370 degrees F for 5 minutes.
6. Spray with oil.
7. Cook for another 5 minutes.

Serving Suggestions: Serve with sweet chili sauce.

Preparation & Cooking Tips: Use lean ground pork.

Buffalo Meatballs

Preparation Time: 20 minutes

Cooking Time: 15 minutes

Servings: 6

Ingredients:

Meatball

- 1 lb. ground beef
- 1 lb. ground pork
- 1 tablespoon onion powder
- 2 eggs, beaten
- ¼ cup milk
- 1 cup Italian breadcrumbs
- 1 tablespoon brown sugar
- 3 tablespoons Parmesan cheese
- 1 teaspoon onion powder
- 1 teaspoon garlic powder
- ½ teaspoon chili powder
- ½ teaspoon smoked paprika
- ½ teaspoon ground cumin
- Salt and pepper to taste

Sauce

- ½ cup hot pepper sauce
- 1 teaspoon garlic powder
- 1 teaspoon onion powder

- Salt and pepper to taste

Method:

1. Combine the meatball ingredients in a bowl.
2. Form meatballs from the mixture.
3. Air fry the meatballs at 400 degrees F for 15 minutes.
4. In a bowl, mix the ingredients for the sauce.
5. Toss the meatballs in the sauce before serving.

Serving Suggestions: Garnish with chopped scallions.

Preparation & Cooking Tips: You can also make the meatballs with ground beef and ground turkey.

Pulled Pork Nachos

Preparation Time: 10 minutes

Cooking Time: 10 minutes

Servings: 6

Ingredients:

- 1 bag nacho chips

Toppings

- 1 cup pulled pork
- ½ cup cucumber, chopped
- ½ cup tomatoes, chopped
- ½ cup olives, pitted and sliced
- 1 tablespoon fresh dill, diced
- ¼ cup feta cheese, crumbled
- ½ cup tzatziki sauce

Method:

1. Arrange the nachos on a baking pan.
2. Top the nachos with the pork, cucumber, tomatoes, olives, dill and cheese.
3. Place the pan in the air fryer.
4. Cook at 320 degrees F for 6 minutes.
5. Drizzle with the sauce before serving.

Serving Suggestions: Garnish with chopped parsley.

Preparation & Cooking Tips: You can also use sliced tortillas in place of the nacho chips.

Salami Chips

Preparation Time: 5 minutes

Cooking Time: 5 minutes

Servings: 6

Ingredients:

- 1 pack salami, sliced thinly

Method:

1. Add the salami slices to the air fryer.
2. Air fry at 350 degrees F for 5 minutes.
3. Drain on a plate lined with paper towel.

Serving Suggestions: Serve with garlic mayo dip.

Preparation & Cooking Tips: Use low-sodium salami.

Bacon-Wrapped Asparagus

Preparation Time: 5 minutes

Cooking Time: 9 minutes

Servings: 4

Ingredients:

- 1 lb. asparagus
- 6 slices bacon

Method:

1. Wrap a bunch of asparagus with bacon.
2. Place in the air fryer basket.
3. Cook at 380 degrees F for 10 minutes, turning once or twice.

Serving Suggestions: Serve with hot pepper sauce.

Preparation & Cooking Tips: Secure bacon with toothpicks.

Honey Glazed Rolls

Preparation Time: 10 minutes

Cooking Time: 5 minutes

Servings: 6

Ingredients:

- 1 pack crescent rolls
- 2 tablespoons honey mustard
- 1 pack cocktail hotdogs

Sauce

- ¼ cup honey mustard
- ¼ cup butter
- 1 teaspoon Worcestershire sauce
- 1 tablespoon brown sugar

Method:

1. Spread the rolls on a plate.
2. Spread honey mustard on top.
3. Slice into 4 pieces.
4. Wrap the sheets around the hotdogs.
5. Place the rolls in the air fryer.
6. Cook at 320 degrees F for 5 minutes.
7. In a pan over medium heat, combine the sauce ingredients.
8. Simmer until sauce has thickened.
9. Serve rolls with sauce.

Serving Suggestions: You can also drizzle with sauce and serve.

Preparation & Cooking Tips: You can also use sliced sausages for this recipe.

Italian Sausage Bites

Preparation Time: 5 minutes

Cooking Time: 10 minutes

Servings: 4

Ingredients:

- 1 lb. Italian sausages
- 2 tablespoons olive oil
- 2 teaspoons dried Italian seasoning

Method:

1. Slice sausages into 3-inch portions.
2. Thread onto toothpicks.
3. Brush with olive oil.
4. Sprinkle with dried Italian herbs.
5. Air fry at 400 degrees F for 5 minutes.

Serving Suggestions: Serve with ketchup and mustard.

Preparation & Cooking Tips: You can also use bratwursts for this recipe.

Calamari

Preparation Time: 5 minutes

Cooking Time: 10 minutes

Servings: 4

Ingredients:

- 1 lb. squid, sliced into rings
- Salt and pepper to taste
- ¼ cup flour
- 2 eggs, beaten
- 1 cup breadcrumbs
- Cooking spray

Method:

1. Season squid with salt and pepper.
2. Coat with flour.
3. Dip in eggs.
4. Cover with breadcrumbs.
5. Spray with oil.
6. Cook at 350 degrees F for 5 minutes per side.

Serving Suggestions: Serve with tartar sauce.

Preparation & Cooking Tips: If you want calamari crispier, cook for another 3 minutes.

Bacon & Shrimp

Preparation Time: 30 minutes

Cooking Time: 10 minutes

Servings: 4

Ingredients:

- 12 shrimp, peeled and deveined
- 12 slices bacon

Method:

1. Preheat your air fryer to 390 degrees F.
2. Wrap shrimp with bacon slices.
3. Add to the air fryer rack.
4. Air fry for 5 minutes per side.

Serving Suggestions: Serve with spicy mayo dip.

Preparation & Cooking Tips: You can also sprinkle shrimp with herbs before wrapping with bacon.

Chapter 10: Egg Recipes

Scotch Eggs

Preparation Time: 5 minutes

Cooking Time: 15 minutes

Servings: 4

Ingredients:

- 1 lb. Italian ground sausage patties
- 4 hard boiled eggs

Method:

1. Roll the sausage patties around the eggs.
2. Place these in the air fryer basket.
3. Cook at 350 degrees F for 15 minutes.

Serving Suggestions: Serve with your favorite condiments.

Preparation & Cooking Tips: You can also make your own sausage patties.

Egg & Cheese Muffin

Preparation Time: 5 minutes

Cooking Time: 7 minutes

Servings: 4

Ingredients:

- Cooking spray
- 4 eggs
- ¼ cup cheese, shredded
- ¼ cup heavy cream
- Salt and pepper to taste

Method:

1. Spray your muffin pan with oil.
2. Beat the eggs in a bowl.
3. Stir in the cheese, cream, salt and pepper.
4. Pour mixture into the muffin cups.
5. Cook in the air fryer at 350 degrees F for 5 to 7 minutes.

Serving Suggestions: Garnish with pepper.

Preparation & Cooking Tips: Use cheddar or gruyere for this recipe.

Baked Eggs

Preparation Time: 5 minutes

Cooking Time: 5 minutes

Servings: 4

Ingredients:

- Cooking spray
- 4 eggs
- 1 teaspoon dried basil
- Salt and pepper to taste

Method:

1. Preheat your air fryer to 300 degrees F.
2. Spray your muffin pan with oil.
3. Crack the eggs into the muffin cups.
4. Season with basil, salt and pepper.
5. Cook at 330 degrees F for 5 minutes.

Serving Suggestions: Let cool before removing from the muffin cups.

Southern Deviled Eggs

Preparation Time: 10 minutes

Cooking Time: 10 minutes

Servings: 12

Ingredients:

- 6 hard boiled eggs, peeled and sliced in half
- 3 tablespoons mayonnaise
- 1 ½ tablespoons sweet pickle relish
- 1 teaspoon mustard
- Salt and pepper to taste

Method:

1. Scoop out the yolks from the eggs.
2. Add the yolks to a bowl.
3. Stir in the rest of the ingredients.
4. Top the egg whites with the mixture.

Serving Suggestions: Sprinkle with paprika before serving.

Preparation & Cooking Tips: Soak the eggs in ice bath to make these easier to peel.

Herbed Baked Eggs

Preparation Time: 5 minutes

Cooking Time: 10 minutes

Servings: 4

Ingredients:

- Cooking spray
- 4 eggs
- Salt and pepper to taste
- ½ tablespoon fresh basil, chopped
- ½ tablespoon fresh thyme, chopped

Method:

1. Spray your muffin pan with oil.
2. Crack the eggs into the muffin cups.
3. Season with salt and pepper.
4. Sprinkle the herbs on top.
5. Place in the air fryer rack.
6. Cook at 350 degrees F for 3 to 5 minutes.

Serving Suggestions: Sprinkle with a little pepper before serving.

Preparation & Cooking Tips: Check eggs for doneness. Cook until set.

Chapter 11: 30-Day Meal Plan

Day 1

Breakfast: Beef & egg rolls

Lunch: Grilled swordfish

Dinner: Country-style steak

Day 2

Breakfast: Bacon burrito

Lunch: Salmon patties

Dinner: Beef liver & onions

Day 3

Breakfast: Ham & egg cups

Lunch: Carne asada

Dinner: Pork teriyaki

Day 4

Breakfast: French toast rolls with sausage

Lunch: Spicy shrimp

Dinner: Garlic& rosemary lamb chops

Day 5

Breakfast: Crispy bacon

Lunch: Steak with chipotle butter

Dinner: Parmesan pork with herbs

Day 6

Breakfast: Breakfast muffin with bacon & eggs

Lunch: Herbed tilapia

Dinner: Roast lamb

Day 7

Breakfast: Sausage patties

Lunch: Blackened shrimp

Dinner: Cheese stuffed meatloaf

Day 8

Breakfast: Maple breakfast sausage

Lunch: Shrimp scampi

Dinner: Flank steak with chimichurri

Day 9

Breakfast: Bacon burrito

Lunch: Crab cakes

Dinner: Lamb with lemon & cumin

Day 10

Breakfast: Sausage & egg bites

Lunch: Grilled swordfish

Dinner: Blackened pork chops

Day 11

Breakfast: Breakfast potatoes with bacon & ham

Lunch: Kielbasa

Dinner: Beef liver & onions

Day 12

Breakfast: Sausage patties

Lunch: Shrimp bang bang

Dinner: Garlic butter steak

Day 13

Breakfast: Beef & egg rolls

Lunch: Carne asada

Dinner: Lamb chops with herb butter

Day 14

Breakfast: Crispy bacon

Lunch: Flank steak with chimichurri

Dinner: Spicy shrimp

Day 15

Breakfast: French toast rolls with sausage

Lunch: Herbed tilapia

Dinner: Honey glazed ham

Day 16

Breakfast: Breakfast potatoes with bacon & ham

Lunch: Salmon with mustard sauce

Dinner: Honey garlic pork chops

Day 17

Breakfast: Ham & egg cups

Lunch: Country-style steak

Dinner: Korean beef short ribs

Day 18

Breakfast: Breakfast muffin with bacon & eggs

Lunch: Blackened shrimp

Dinner: Steak with chipotle butter

Day 19

Breakfast: Maple breakfast sausage

Lunch: Barbecue pork

Dinner: Garlic butter steak

Day 20

Breakfast: Sausage & egg bites

Lunch: Cheese stuffed meatloaf

Dinner: Italian lamb chops

Day 21

Breakfast: Breakfast potatoes with bacon & ham

Lunch: Honey lemon salmon

Dinner: Rib eye steak with blue cheese sauce

Day 22

Breakfast: Sausage patties

Lunch: Lamb chops with horseradish sauce

Dinner: Crispy pork belly

Day 23

Breakfast: Bacon burrito

Lunch: Salmon with mustard sauce

Dinner: Greek lamb chops

Day 24

Breakfast: Beef & egg rolls

Lunch: Honey lemon salmon

Dinner: Apricot pork chops

Day 25

Breakfast: Sausage & egg bites

Lunch: Shrimp bang bang

Dinner: Lamb with lemon & coriander

Day 26

Breakfast: Maple breakfast sausage

Lunch: Crab cakes

Dinner: Korean beef short ribs

Day 27

Breakfast: French toast rolls with sausage

Lunch: Mint lamb

Dinner: Salmon patties

Day 28

Breakfast: Ham & egg cups

Lunch: Crispy pork belly

Dinner: Rib eye steak with blue cheese sauce

Day 29

Breakfast: Breakfast muffin with bacon & eggs

Lunch: Garlic mustard steak

Dinner: Breaded pork chops

Day 30

Breakfast: Crispy bacon

Lunch: Beef liver & onions

Dinner: Herbed rack of lamb

Conclusion

The Carnivore diet is an eating plan that has a lot of potential health benefits. It is certainly one of the more radical approaches as it requires nourishment from only meat and animal products. Many dieters who have taken on the carnivorous diet have reported positive impacts on their overall health.

Air fryers are compact kitchen appliances that are can air fry, toast, roast, bake, and broil. Perhaps one of the best things about air fryers is that you can still indulge in fried food while on a restrictive diet. They are superb at cooking delicious food rapidly and with little supervision. Air fryers are excellent options for those on a carnivore diet. Whether it is steak, burger, or fish, air fryers are more than capable of cooking meats beautifully and flavorfully.

Printed in the USA
CPSIA information can be obtained
at www.ICGtesting.com
LVHW081150270224
772718LV00033B/212

9 781954 091405